English - Urdu

Vocabulary building is crucial for children as it improves communication skills, comprehension and academic success. This is a gradual process and using this book can be a great starting point for your children.

To build vocabulary, read together, play word games, practice with flashcards, encourage writing, use words in daily life, review regularly. It is essential to be patient and persistent with your child as he learns new words.

To watch the video alongside this book, simply go to the website provided on the last page. You can freely access it as per your convenience. Let's start!

whale

وہیل

SUBSCRIBE

Lifetime Access !!!

duck #1	starfish #2	octopus #3	eagle #4

بطخ	ستارہ مچھلی	آکٹوپس	عقاب

dinosaur #5	oyster #6	lizard #7	cat #8

ڈائناسور	صدف	چھپکلی	بلی

centipede #9	monkey #10	dove #11	goose #12

کنکھجورا	بندر	کبوتر	بطخ

porcupine #13	mosquito #14	mare #15	lion #16

سیہہ	مچھر	گھوڑی	شیر

insect #17	seagull #18	mice #19	toad #20

کیڑا	سمندری بگلا	چوہے	مینڈک

snail #21	boar #22	squirrel #23	hippopotamus #24

گھونگا	جنگلی سور	گلہری	دریائی گھوڑا

rooster #25	snake #26	ostrich #27	shark #28

مرغ	سانپ	شترمرغ	شارک

chicken #29	hedgehog #30	cheetah #31	goat #32

مرغی	ہیج ہاگ	چیتا	بکری

#33 vulture

گدھ

#34 camel

اونٹ

#35 rat

چوہا

#36 cow

گائے

#37 cockroach

لال بیگ

#38 ant

چیونٹی

#39 kangaroo

کینگارو

#40 caterpillar

کیٹرپلر

#41 rabbit

خرگوش

#42 unicorn

یونیکورن

#43 turtle

کچھوا

#44 owl

الو

#45 frog

مینڈک

#46 fish

مچھلی

#47 moth

پتنگا

#48 clam

صدف

#49 grasshopper	#50 spider	#51 jellyfish	#52 parrot
ٹڈّی	مکڑی	جیلی فش	طوطا

#53 swan	#54 elephant	#55 puppy	#56 turkey
ہنس	ہاتھی	کتّا کا بچّہ	ترکی

#57 dog	#58 peacock	#59 deer	#60 mouse
کتا	مور	ہرن	چوہا

#61 hen	#62 monster	#63 reindeer	#64 beetle
مرغی	عفریت	بارہ سنگھا	بھونرا

#65 bird	#66 stork	#67 mermaid	#68 alligator
پرندہ	سارس	جل پری	مگرمچھ

#69 dragonfly	#70 squid	#71 sparrow	#72 kitten
ڈریگن فلائی	اسکوئڈ	چڑیا	بلی کا بچہ

#73 worm	#74 hawk	#75 crab	#76 sheep
کیڑا	شاہین	کیکڑا	بھیڑ

#77 quail	#78 pelican	#79 pigeon	#80 lobster
بٹیر	پیلیکن	کبوتر	لوبسٹر

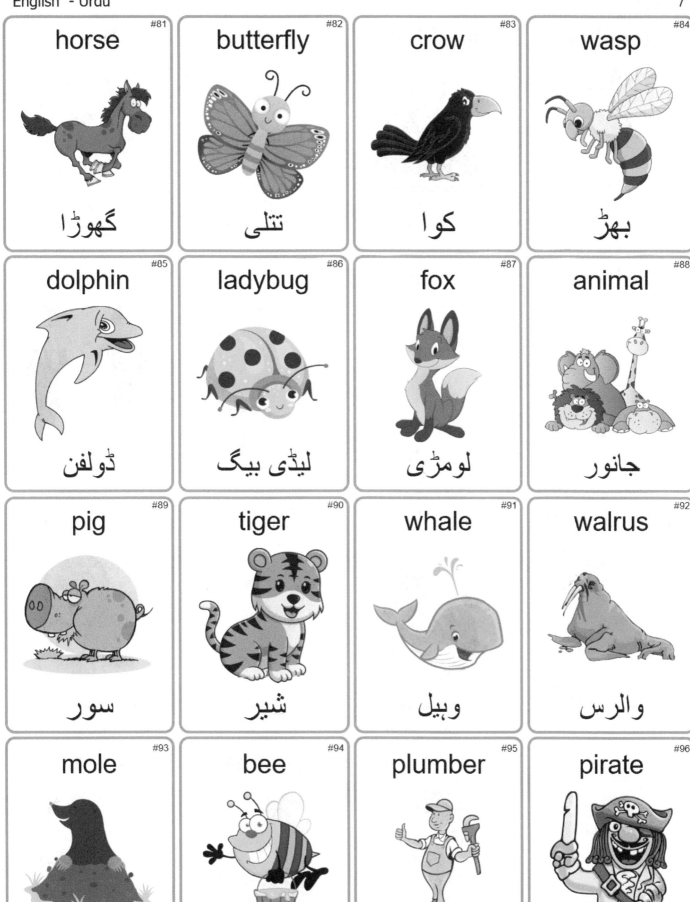

#81 horse	#82 butterfly	#83 crow	#84 wasp
گھوڑا	تتلی	کوا	بھِڑ

#85 dolphin	#86 ladybug	#87 fox	#88 animal
ڈولفن	لیڈی بیگ	لومڑی	جانور

#89 pig	#90 tiger	#91 whale	#92 walrus
سور	شیر	وہیل	والرس

#93 mole	#94 bee	#95 plumber	#96 pirate
تل	مکھی	پلمبر	سمندری ڈاکو

#97 teacher	#98 president	#99 musician	#100 baker
استاد	صدر	موسیقار	نانبائی

#101 butcher	#102 singer	#103 chef	#104 lawyer
قصائی	گلوکار	شیف	وکیل

#105 accountant	#106 knight	#107 farmer	#108 pharmacist
اکاؤنٹنٹ	شہسوار	کسان	فارماسسٹ

#109 angel	#110 army	#111 optician	#112 fisherman
فرشتہ	فوج	آپٹیشین	ماہی گیر

#113 entrepreneur	#114 secretary	#115 princess	#116 ghost

کاروباری شخص	سیکریٹری	شہزادی	بھوت

#117 carpenter	#118 photographer	#119 doctor	#120 cashier

بڑھئی	فوٹوگرافر	ڈاکٹر	کیشئر

#121 waiter	#122 bartender	#123 boss	#124 queen

ویٹر	بارٹینڈر	باس	ملکہ

#125 barber	#126 leader	#127 hairdresser	#128 driver

نائی	رہنما	حجام	ڈرائیور

#129 **bishop**  پادری	#130 **nurse**  نرس	#131 **miner**  کان کن	#132 **maid**  ملازمہ
#133 **writer**  مصنف	#134 **police**  پولیس	#135 **artist**  آرٹسٹ	#136 **politician**  سیاست دان
#137 **florist**  پھول فروش	#138 **actor**  اداکار	#139 **magician**  جادوگر	#140 **cop** پولیس اہلکار
#141 **judge**  جج	#142 **witch**  چڑیل	#143 **receptionist**  ریسپشنسٹ	#144 **veterinarian**  جانوروں کا ڈاکٹر

policeman #145

پولیس مین

king #146

بادشاہ

red #147

سرخ

white #148

color the word and
the picture in pink

سفید

pink #149

color the word and
the picture in pink

گلابی

blue #150

color the word and
the picture in pink

نیلا

gray #151

color the word and
the picture in pink

سرمئی

yellow #152

color the word and
the picture in pink

پیلا

brown #153

color the word and
the picture in pink

بھورا

green #154

color the word and
the picture in pink

سبز

children #155

بچے

family #156

خاندان

granddaughter #157

پوتی

wife #158

بیوی

daughter #159

بیٹی

girlfriend #160

گرل فرینڈ

#161 father باپ	#162 friend دوست	#163 woman عورت	#164 cousin کزن
#165 stepmother سوتیلی ماں	#166 boyfriend بوائے فرینڈ	#167 mom ماں	#168 kid بچہ
#169 lady خاتون	#170 sister بہن	#171 dad والد	#172 people لوگ
#173 grandson پوتا	#174 brother بھائی	#175 stepdaughter سوتیلی بیٹی	#176 uncle چاچا

#177 nephew	#178 kids	#179 child	#180 aunt

بھتیجا	بچے	بچہ	خالہ

#181 toddler	#182 son	#183 group	#184 stepson

ننھا بچہ	بیٹا	گروپ	سوتیلا بیٹا

#185 girl	#186 member	#187 mother	#188 boy

لڑکی	رکن	ماں	لڑکا

#189 man	#190 grandmother	#191 niece	#192 briefcase

آدمی	دادی	بھتیجی	بریف کیس

#193 silk	#194 dress	#195 stockings	#196 spoon

ریشم	لباس	موزے	چمچ

#197 hat	#198 skirt	#199 underpants	#200 necklace
			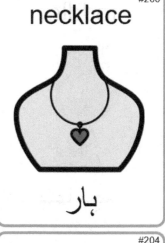
ٹوپی	اسکرٹ	انڈرپینٹس	ہار

#201 glass	#202 kitchen	#203 shoes	#204 mirror

شیشہ	باورچی خانہ	جوتے	آئینہ

#205 teacup	#206 refrigerator	#207 seeds	#208 engine

چائے کا کپ	فریج	بیج	انجن

cleanser #209

صفائی کرنے والا

alcohol #210

الکحل

oven #211

تندور

newspaper #212
اخبار

notebook #213

نوٹ بک

dice #214
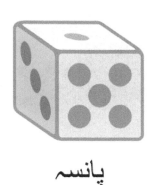
پانسہ

belt #215

بیلٹ

towel #216

تولیہ

scarf #217

مفلر

pacifier #218

چوسنی

television #219

ٹیلیویژن

fireplace #220

آتش دان

socks #221
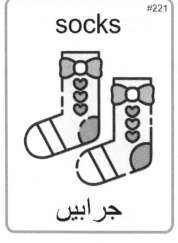
جرابیں

magazine #222

رسالہ

carpet #223

قالین

picture #224

تصویر

#225 fork	#226 bed	#227 paper	#228 strainer

کانٹا	بستر	کاغذ	چھلنی

#229 pin	#230 hanger	#231 money	#232 lid

پن	ہینگر	پیسہ	ڈھکن

#233 tire	#234 dictionary	#235 dish	#236 cage

ٹائر	لغت	پلیٹ	پنجرا

#237 pajamas	#238 bedroom	#239 crayon	#240 toothbrush
			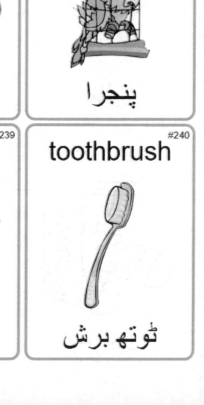
پاجامہ	بیڈروم	رنگین پنسل	ٹوتھ برش

kettle #241

کیتلی

candle #242

موم بتی

clothes #243
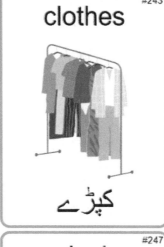
کپڑے

wrench #244

رینچ

shovel #245

بیلچہ

closet #246

الماری

clock #247

گھڑی

apron #248

ایپرن

compass #249

قطب نما

oil #250

تیل

gift #251

تحفہ

saucer #252

پلیٹ

bucket #253

بالٹی

bottle #254

بوتل

brush #255

برش

bouquet #256

گلدستہ

jacket #257

جیکٹ

raincoat #258

برساتی

broom #259

جھاڑو

rope #260

رسی

flag #261

جھنڈا

diaper #262

ڈائپر

bell #263

گھنٹی

vest #264

بنیان

ink #265

سیاہی

blanket #266

کمبل

stapler #267

اسٹپلر

chainsaw #268

چینسا

basket #269

ٹوکری

umbrella #270

چھتری

cot #271

چارپائی

collar #272
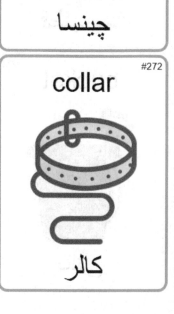
کالر

#273 shirt — قمیض	#274 telescope — دوربین	#275 bin — کوڑے دان	#276 phone — فون
#277 plate — پلیٹ	#278 bathtub — باتھ ٹب	#279 bassinet — جھولا	#280 ladder — سیڑھی
#281 chalkboard — بلیک بورڈ	#282 pen — قلم	#283 eraser — ربڑ	#284 slippers — چپل
#285 metal — دھات	#286 bracelet — کنگن	#287 coat — کوٹ	#288 pillow — تکیہ

#289 syringe	#290 cupboard	#291 yarn	#292 pliers
سرنج	برتنوں کی الماری	اون	چمٹا
#293 paintbrush	**#294 calculator**	**#295 toilet**	**#296 tent**
پینٹ برش	کیلکولیٹر	بیت الخلاء	خیمہ
#297 glove	**#298 bookcase**	**#299 desk**	**#300 cabinet**
دستانے	کتابوں کی الماری	ڈیسک	الماری
#301 stove	**#302 trousers**	**#303 lantern**	**#304 prize**
چولہا	پتلون	لالٹین	انعام

letter #305  خط	table #306  میز	fan #307  پنکھا	bookshelf #308  کتابوں کی الماری
razor #309  استرا	pitcher #310  گھڑا	mask #311  ماسک	napkin #312  رومال
mug #313  پیالا	torch #314  مشعل	tool #315  اوزار	calendar #316  کیلنڈر
typewriter #317  ٹائپ رائٹر	map #318  نقشہ	toy #319  کھلونا	rake #320  ریک

| #321 earring | #322 pearls | #323 suitcase | #324 pan |
| بالیاں | موتی | سوٹ کیس | پین |

| #325 mat | #326 lipstick | #327 undershirt | #328 cushion |
| چٹائی | لپ اسٹک | انڈرشِرٹ | کشن |

| #329 device | #330 chair | #331 telephone | #332 jug |
| آلہ | کرسی | ٹیلیفون | گھڑا |

| #333 window | #334 key | #335 doll | #336 backpack |
| کھڑکی | چابی | گڑیا | بیگ پیک |

#337	#338	#339	#340
cup	box	teapot	bowtie
کپ	ڈبہ	چائے کی کیتلی	بو ٹائی

#341	#342	#343	#344
sweater	bowl	scissors	lamp
سویٹر	پیالہ	قینچی	چراغ

#345	#346	#347	#348
book	pants	rug	comb
کتاب	پتلون	قالین	کنگھی

#349	#350	#351	#352
cactus	microscope	handkerchief	microphone
کیکٹس	خوردبین	رومال	مائیکروفون

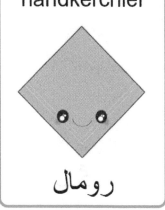

#353 bomb	#354 cap	#355 equipment	#356 machine

بم	ٹوپی	آلات	مشین

#357 knife	#358 ax	#359 wreath	#360 wood

چاقو	کلہاڑی	پھولوں کا ہار	لکڑی

#361 screwdriver	#362 ruler	#363 helmet	#364 shorts

پچکس	پیمانہ	ہیلمٹ	نیکر

#365 cash	#366 bag	#367 tray	#368 utensils
		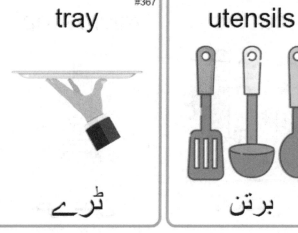	
نقد	بیگ	ٹرے	برتن

#369 crayons	#370 pot	#371 photo	#372 soap

رنگین پنسل	برتن	تصویر	صابن

#373 pencil	#374 gasoline	#375 lightbulb	#376 curtains

پنسل	پٹرول	بلب	پردے

#377 gun	#378 diamond	#379 toothpaste	#380 spatula

بندوق	ہیرا	ٹوتھ پیسٹ	چمچ

#381 camera	#382 barrel	#383 boot	#384 vaccine

کیمرہ	بیرل	بوٹ	ویکسین

wallet #385	dust #386	puddle #387	trash #388

بٹوہ	دھول	تالاب	کوڑا

bridge #389	tree #390	area #391	field #392
		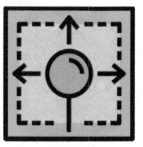	
پل	درخت	علاقہ	میدان

chimney #393	gravel #394	windmill #395	gate #396

چمنی	بجری	ہوا چکی	دروازہ

bathroom #397	farm #398	tombstone #399	palm #400

بیت الخلا	کھیت	قبر کا کتبہ	کھجور

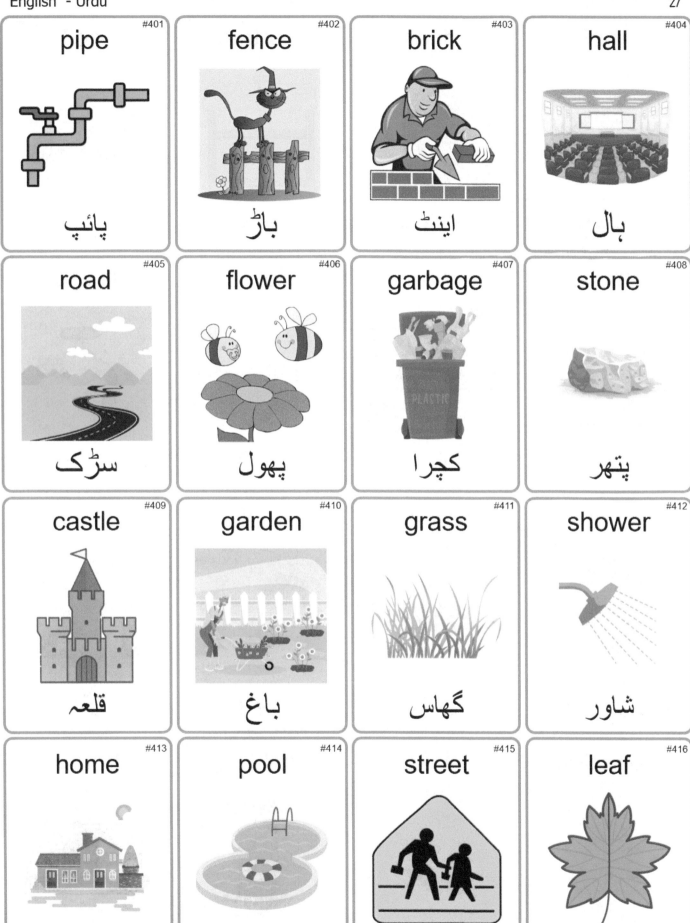

pipe #401	fence #402	brick #403	hall #404
پائپ	باڑ	اینٹ	ہال
road #405	flower #406	garbage #407	stone #408
سڑک	پھول	کچرا	پتھر
castle #409	garden #410	grass #411	shower #412
قلعہ	باغ	گھاس	شاور
home #413	pool #414	street #415	leaf #416
گھر	تالاب	سڑک	پتی

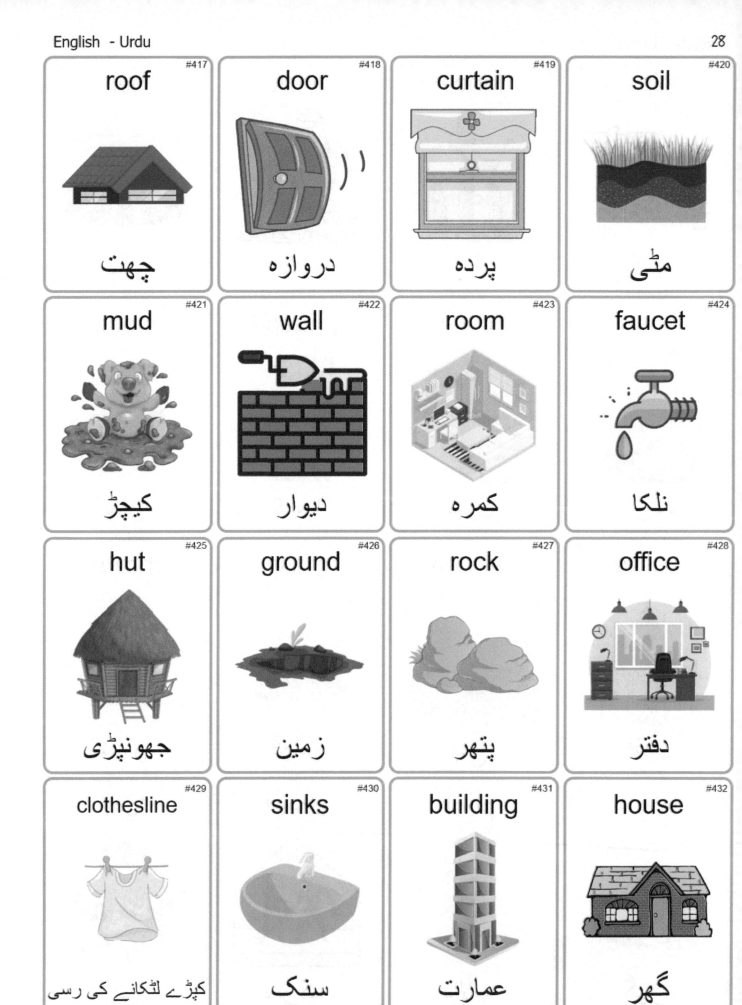

#417 roof چھت	#418 door دروازہ	#419 curtain پردہ	#420 soil مٹی
#421 mud کیچڑ	#422 wall دیوار	#423 room کمرہ	#424 faucet نلکا
#425 hut جھونپڑی	#426 ground زمین	#427 rock پتھر	#428 office دفتر
#429 clothesline کپڑے لٹکانے کی رسی	#430 sinks سنک	#431 building عمارت	#432 house گھر

shelter #433	**crawl** #434	**smell** #435	**nap** #436

پناہ	رینگنا	سونگھنا	جھپکی
boil #437	**solve** #438	**prefer** #439	**hurt** #440

ابالنا	حل	ترجیح دیں	تکلیف
kiss #441	**follow** #442	**come** #443	**bite** #444

چومنا	پیروی کرنا	آؤ	کاٹنا
discuss #445	**dig** #446	**respect** #447	**sleep** #448

بحث کرنا	کھودنا	عزت	سونا

#449 sick بیمار	#450 run دوڑنا	#451 listen سننا	#452 beg بھیک مانگنا
#453 sketch خاکہ	#454 angry غصہ	#455 receive وصول کرنا	#456 cut کاٹنا
#457 close بند کرنا	#458 fry تلنا	#459 cry رونا	#460 give دینا
#461 prevent روکنا	#462 rob ڈاکہ ڈالنا	#463 bake بیک کرنا	#464 speak بولنا

#465 buy	#466 knit	#467 create	#468 win
خریدنا	بُننا	بنانا	جیتتنا

#469 read	#470 meet	#471 enjoy	#472 remember
پڑھنا	ملنا	لطف اندوز ہونا	یاد رکھنا

#473 wag	#474 develop	#475 forbid	#476 bathe
دم ہلانا	ترقی کرنا	منع کرنا	غسل کرنا

#477 nibble	#478 sit	#479 cook	#480 drink

نبل	بیٹھنا	کھانا پکانا	پینا

#481 smile	#482 hello	#483 hug	#484 improve

مسکراہٹ	ہیلو	گلے لگانا	بہتر بنانا

#485 prepare	#486 climb	#487 dream	#488 drill

تیاری کرنا	چڑھنا	خواب دیکھنا	ڈرل

#489 race	#490 help	#491 invest	#492 clean

دوڑ	مدد	سرمایہ کاری کرنا	صفائی کرنا

#493 decrease	#494 think	#495 jump	#496 understand

کمی	سوچنا	چھلانگ لگانا	سمجھنا

fly #497	**discover** #498	**build** #499	**believe** #500
اڑنا	دریافت کرنا	تعمیر	یقین
roast #501	**tame** #502	**sing** #503	**shake** #504
بھونا	سدھانا	گانا	ہلانا
love #505	**play** #506	**clap** #507	**teach** #508
محبت	کھیلنا	تالیاں بجانا	پڑھانا
grill #509	**sew** #510	**write** #511	**celebrate** #512
گرل کرنا	سلائی کرنا	لکھنا	جشن منانا

#513 snore	#514 grow	#515 stop	#516 walk

خراٹے لینا	بڑھنا	رکنا	چلنا

#517 wait	#518 wash	#519 thank	#520 eat

انتظار کرنا	دھونا	شکریہ	کھانا

#521 protect	#522 open	#523 achieve	#524 hide

تحفظ کرنا	کھولنا	حاصل کرنا	چھپانا

#525 avoid	#526 goodbye	#527 laugh	#528 talk

پرہیز کرنا	خدا حافظ	ہنسنا	بات کرنا

| #529 choose | #530 violin | #531 drum | #532 music |
| چننا | وائلن | ڈھول | موسیقی |

| #533 piano | #534 guitar | #535 zero | #536 one |
| پیانو | گٹار | صفر | ایک |

| #537 two | #538 three | #539 four | #540 five |
| دو | تین | چار | پانچ |

| #541 six | #542 seven | #543 eight | #544 nine |
| چھ | سات | آٹھ | نو |

#545	#546	#547	#548
ten	eleven	twelve	thirteen

| دس | گیاره | باره | تیره |

#549	#550	#551	#552
fourteen	fifteen	sixteen	seventeen

| چوده | پندره | سولہ | ستره |

#553	#554	#555	#556
eighteen	nineteen	twenty	twenty one

| اٹھاره | انیس | بیس | اکیس |

#557	#558	#559	#560
twenty two	twenty three	twenty four	twenty five

| بائیس | تئیس | چوبیس | پچیس |

#561 twenty six	#562 twenty seven	#563 twenty eight	#564 twenty nine
26 چھبیس	**27** ستائیس	**28** اٹھائیس	**29** انتیس
#565 thirty	#566 thirty one	#567 thirty two	#568 thirty three
30 تیس	**31** اکتیس	**32** بتیس	**33** تینتیس
#569 thirty four	#570 thirty five	#571 thirty six	#572 thirty seven
34 چونتیس	**35** پینتیس	**36** چھتیس	**37** سینتیس
#573 thirty eight	#574 thirty nine	#575 forty	#576 forty one
38 اٹھتیس	**39** انتالیس	**40** چالیس	**41** اکتالیس

#577 forty two	#578 forty three	#579 forty four	#580 forty five
42	43	44	45
بیالیس	تینتالیس	چوالیس	پینتالیس

#581 forty six	#582 forty seven	#583 forty eight	#584 forty nine
46	47	48	49
چھیالیس	سینتالیس	اڑتالیس	اننچاس

#585 fifty	#586 fifty one	#587 fifty two	#588 fifty three
50	51	52	53
پچاس	اکیاون	باون	ترپن

#589 fifty four	#590 fifty five	#591 fifty six	#592 fifty seven
54	55	56	57
چون	پچپن	چھپن	ستاون

fifty eight #593	**fifty nine** #594	**sixty** #595	**sixty one** #596
58	59	60	61
اٹھاون	انسٹھ	ساٹھ	اکسٹھ
sixty two #597	**sixty three** #598	**sixty four** #599	**sixty five** #600
62	63	64	65
باسٹھ	تریسٹھ	چونسٹھ	پینسٹھ
sixty six #601	**sixty seven** #602	**sixty eight** #603	**sixty nine** #604
66	67	68	69
چھیاسٹھ	سرسٹھ	اڑسٹھ	انہتر
seventy #605	**seventy one** #606	**seventy two** #607	**seventy three** #608
70	71	72	73
ستر	اکہتر	بہتر	تہتر

#609 seventy four	#610 seventy five	#611 seventy six	#612 seventy seven
74	75	76	77
چوہتر	پچھتر	چھہتر	ستتر

#613 seventy eight	#614 seventy nine	#615 eighty	#616 eighty one
78	79	80	81
اٹھتر	اناسی	اسی	اکاسی

#617 eighty two	#618 eighty three	#619 eighty four	#620 eighty five
82	83	84	85
بیاسی	تراسی	چوراسی	پچاسی

#621 eighty six	#622 eighty seven	#623 eighty eight	#624 eighty nine
86	87	88	89
چھیاسی	ستاسی	اٹھاسی	نواسی

#625 ninety	#626 ninety one	#627 ninety two	#628 ninety three
90	91	92	93
نوے	اکانوے	بانوے	ترانوے

#629 ninety four	#630 ninety five	#631 ninety six	#632 ninety seven
94	95	96	97
چورانوے	پچانوے	چھیانوے	ستانوے

#633 ninety eight	#634 ninety nine	#635 hundred	#636 thousand
98	99	100	1000
اٹھانوے	ننانوے	سو	ہزار

#637 garlic	#638 icecream	#639 egg	#640 tuna

لہسن	آئس کریم	انڈہ	ٹونا

#641 juice	#642 broccoli	#643 food	#644 apple
رس	بروکلی	کھانا	سیب

#645 apricot	#646 eggplant	#647 celery	#648 peanut
خوبانی	بینگن	اجوائن	مونگ پھلی

#649 shrimp	#650 breakfast	#651 vegetable	#652 seafood
جھینگا	ناشتہ	سبزی	سمندری غذا

#653 wine	#654 jam	#655 pumpkin	#656 soup
شراب	جام	کدو	سوپ

#657	#658	#659	#660
peas	carrot	noodles	pie

مٹر	گاجر	نوڈلز	پائی

#661	#662	#663	#664
sugar	grape	milk	onion
		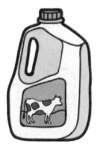	
چینی	انگور	دودھ	پیاز

#665	#666	#667	#668
dinner	rice	tomato	cheese

رات کا کھانا	چاول	ٹماٹر	پنیر

#669	#670	#671	#672
pineapple	lemonade	sausage	salt

اناناس	لیمونیڈ	ساسیج	نمک

sunflower #673

سورج مکھی

cookie #674

بسکٹ

lemon #675

لیموں

spinach #676

پالک

meal #677

کھانا

honey #678

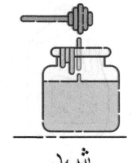

شہد

bean #679

لوبیا

wheat #680

گندم

lychee #681

لیچی

yogurt #682

دہی

pepper #683

کالی مرچ

potato #684

آلو

radish #685

مولی

strawberry #686

اسٹرابیری

pomegranate #687

انار

tea #688

چائے

water #689	**popsicles** #690	**fruit** #691	**cabbage** #692

پانی	آئس لولی	پھل	گوبھی
raspberry #693	**chocolate** #694	**salad** #695	**meat** #696

رسبیری	چاکلیٹ	سلاد	گوشت
coffee #697	**turnip** #698	**pear** #699	**mushroom** #700

کافی	شلجم	ناشپاتی	کھمبی
lettuce #701	**candy** #702	**beer** #703	**cake** #704

سلاد پتہ	ٹافی	بیئر	کیک

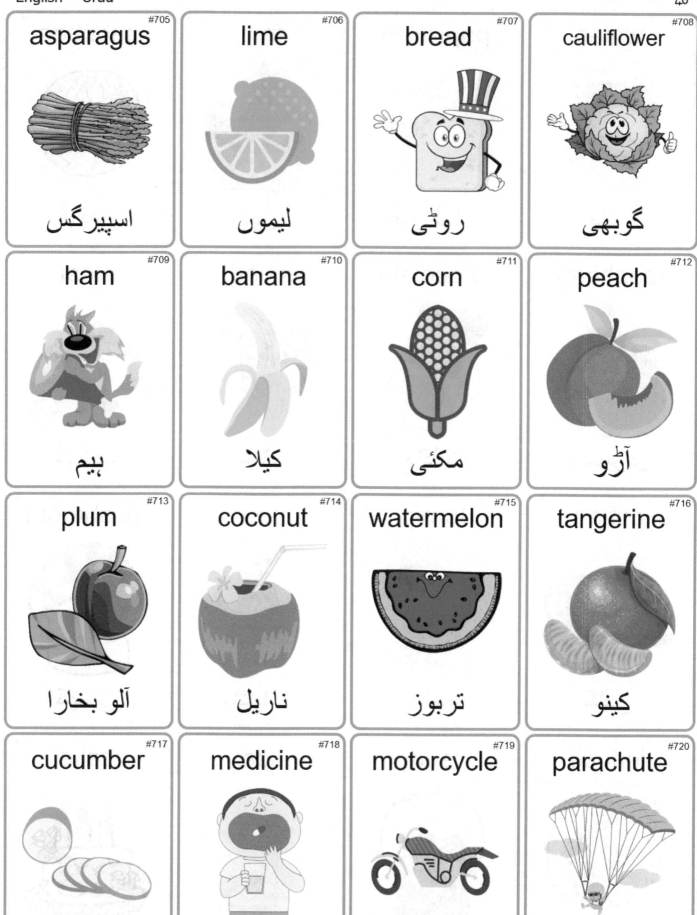

#705 asparagus	#706 lime	#707 bread	#708 cauliflower
اسپیرگس	لیموں	روٹی	گوبھی

#709 ham	#710 banana	#711 corn	#712 peach
ہیم	کیلا	مکئی	آڑو

#713 plum	#714 coconut	#715 watermelon	#716 tangerine
آلو بخارا	ناریل	تربوز	کینو

#717 cucumber	#718 medicine	#719 motorcycle	#720 parachute
کھیرا	دوائی	موٹر سائیکل	پیراشوٹ

#721 barrow	#722 truck	#723 subway	#724 airplane
ریڑھی	ٹرک	سب وے	ہوائی جہاز

#725 boat	#726 ship	#727 vehicle	#728 plane
کشتی	جہاز	گاڑی	جہاز

#729 wagon	#730 train	#731 bicycle	#732 car
بیل گاڑی	ٹرین	سائیکل	گاڑی

#733 ferry	#734 scooter	#735 submarine	#736 helicopter
فیری	اسکوٹر	آبدوز	ہیلی کاپٹر

#737 rocket	#738 sailboat	#739 knees	#740 hip
راکٹ	بادبانی کشتی	گھٹنے	کولہا

#741 eye	#742 teeth	#743 tongue	#744 brain
آنکھ	دانت	زبان	دماغ

#745 nose	#746 body	#747 cheeks	#748 feet
ناک	جسم	گال	پاؤں

#749 glue	#750 mouth	#751 shoulder	#752 tail
گوند	منہ	کندھا	دم

#753 muscle پٹھا	#754 heart دل	#755 toes پیر کی انگلیاں	#756 hips کولہے
#757 bone ہڈی	#758 elbow کہنی	#759 hands ہاتھ	#760 legs ٹانگیں
#761 chin ٹھوڑی	#762 foot پاؤں	#763 throat گلا	#764 beard داڑھی
#765 lips ہونٹ	#766 chest چھاتی	#767 leg ٹانگ	#768 face چہرہ

#769	#770	#771	#772
wig	hair	stomach	neck

وگ	بال	پیٹ	گردن

#773	#774	#775	#776
wing	waist	tooth	ear

پر	کمر	دانت	کان

#777	#778	#779	#780
thumb	forehead	blood	head

انگوٹھا	پیشانی	خون	سر

#781	#782	#783	#784
fin	eyebrows	shoulders	football

پنکھ	ابرو	کندھے	فٹبال

#785	#786	#787	#788
team	fishing	dive	fight
ٹیم	ماہی گیری	غوطہ لگانا	لڑائی

#789	#790	#791	#792
hopping	driving	racket	ride
کودنا	ڈرائیونگ	ریکیٹ	سواری

#793	#794	#795	#796
timer	soccer	dance	boxing
ٹائمر	فٹ بال	ناچنا	باکسنگ

#797	#798	#799	#800
jogging	archery	dumbbells	swimming
ٹہلنا	تیر اندازی	ڈمبل	تیراکی

#801 cycling	#802 gymnastics	#803 wrestling	#804 surfing

سائیکلنگ	جمناسٹک	ریسلنگ	سرفنگ

#805 kite	#806 climbing	#807 friday	#808 wednesday

پتنگ	چڑھنا	جمعہ	بدھ

#809 monday	#810 sunday	#811 tuesday	#812 thursday

پیر	اتوار	منگل	جمعرات

#813 saturday	#814 unhappy	#815 shy	#816 good

ہفتہ	ناخوش	شرمیلا	اچھا

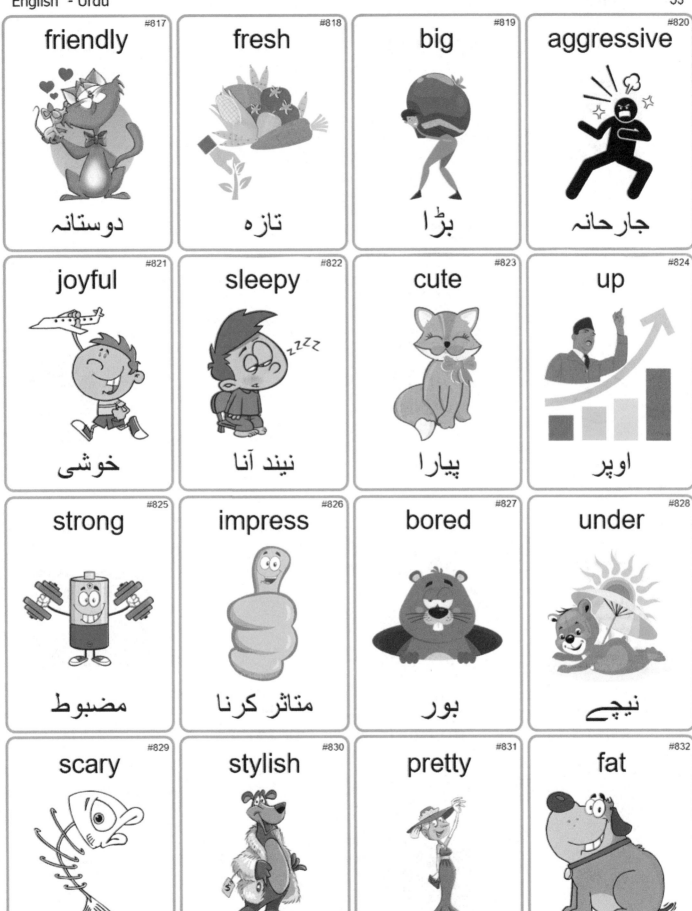

#817 friendly	#818 fresh	#819 big	#820 aggressive
دوستانہ	تازہ	بڑا	جارحانہ

#821 joyful	#822 sleepy	#823 cute	#824 up
خوشی	نیند آنا	پیارا	اوپر

#825 strong	#826 impress	#827 bored	#828 under
مضبوط	متاثر کرنا	بور	نیچے

#829 scary	#830 stylish	#831 pretty	#832 fat
خوفناک	سجیلا	خوبصورت	موٹا

sad #833 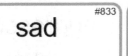 اداس	**smelling** #834  سونگھنا	**mad** #835  پاگل	**proud** #836  فخر
stinky #837  بدبو دار	**happy** #838  خوش	**delicious** #839  مزیدار	**bad** #840  برا
stack #841  ڈھیر لگانا	**profit** #842  منافع	**fact** #843  حقیقت	**data** #844  ڈیٹا
exam #845  امتحان	**evil** #846  برائی	**wealth** #847  دولت	**freedom** #848  آزادی

energy #849  توانائی	**safety** #850  حفاظت	**question** #851  سوال	**technology** #852  ٹیکنالوجی
revenue #853  آمدنی	**history** #854  تاریخ	**activity** #855  سرگرمی	**education** #856  تعلیم
economics #857  معاشیات	**investment** #858  سرمایہ کاری	**direction** #859 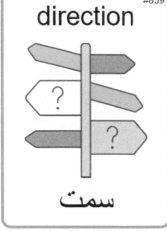 سمت	**goal** #860  مقصد
theory #861 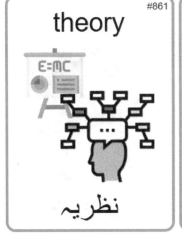 نظریہ	**friendship** #862  دوستی	**entertainment** #863  تفریح	**society** #864  معاشرہ

anxiety #865	**health** #866	**security** #867	**knowledge** #868
اضطراب	صحت	سلامتی	علم
idea #869	**ability** #870	**summer** #871	**snowy** #872
خیال	صلاحیت	گرمیوں کا موسم	برفانی
atmosphere #873	**disaster** #874	**rainbow** #875	**snow** #876
ماحول	آفت	قوس قزح	برف
coast #877	**foggy** #878	**nature** #879	**quiet** #880
ساحل	دھندلا	فطرت	خاموش

#881 moon چاند	#882 rainy بارش والا	#883 wave لہر	#884 world دنیا
#885 mountain پہاڑ	#886 sun سورج	#887 steam بھاپ	#888 sea سمندر
#889 river دریا	#890 earth زمین	#891 sunny دھوپ والا	#892 star ستارہ
#893 smoke دھواں	#894 rain بارش	#895 location مقام	#896 cloudy ابر آلود

snowflake #897	**loud** #898	**cold** #899	**dawn** #900

برف کا ٹکڑا	اونچی آواز	سرد	طلوع فجر
hot #901	**windy** #902	**volcano** #903	**sound** #904

گرم	ہوا دار	آتش فشاں	آواز
wet #905	**heat** #906	**lake** #907	**humid** #908

گیلا	گرمی	جھیل	مرطوب
temperature #909	**climate** #910	**thunder** #911	**stormy** #912

درجہ حرارت	آب و ہوا	گرج	طوفانی

#913 year	#914 night	#915 noon	#916 month

سال	رات	دوپہر	مہینہ

#917 midnight	#918 day	#919 week	#920 morning

آدھی رات	دن	ہفتہ	صبح

#921 date	#922 autumn	#923 time	#924 birthday

تاریخ	خزاں	وقت	سالگرہ

#925 country	#926 income	#927 product	#928 square
			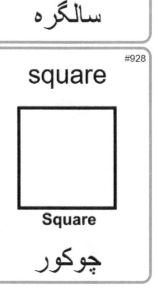
ملک	آمدنی	مصنوعات	چوکور

#929 war	#930 customer	#931 math	#932 number

جنگ	گاہک	ریاضی	نمبر

#933 bubble	#934 winner	#935 song	#936 story

بلبلہ	فاتح	گانا	کہانی

#937 sculpture	#938 painting	#939 movie	#940 user

مجسمہ	پینٹنگ	فلم	صارف

#941 homework	#942 ice	#943 chemistry	#944 game

ہوم ورک	برف	کیمسٹری	کھیل

#945 company	#946 pair	#947 funeral	#948 worker

کمپنی	جوڑی	جنازہ	مزدور

#949 disease	#950 government	#951 signature	#952 cube
			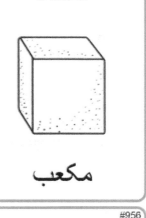
بیماری	حکومت	دستخط	مکعب

#953 message	#954 news	#955 language	#956 christmas

پیغام	خبریں	زبان	کرسمس

#957 wheel	#958 art	#959 package	#960 circle

پہیہ	فن	پیکج	دائرہ

#961 arrow	#962 triangle	#963 wedding	#964 error
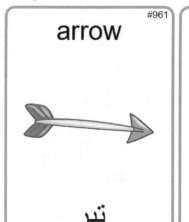			
تیر	مثلث	شادی	غلطی

#965 point	#966 debt	#967 dirt	#968 paint

نقطہ	قرض	گندگی	پینٹ

#969 octagon	#970 passenger	#971 fire	#972 law

آٹھ کونوں والا	مسافر	آگ	قانون

#973 industry	#974 scale	#975 school	#976 hill

صنعت	پیمانہ	اسکول	پہاڑی

#977 estate	#978 apartment	#979 island	#980 highway

جائیداد	اپارٹمنٹ	جزیرہ	ہائی وے

#981 lighthouse	#082 village	#983 hospital	#984 cafe

لائٹ ہاؤس	گاؤں	ہسپتال	کیفے

#985 desert	#986 university	#987 airport	#988 beach

صحرا	یونیورسٹی	ہوائی اڈہ	ساحل

#989 classroom	#990 market	#991 town	#992 jungle

کلاس روم	مارکیٹ	قصبہ	جنگل

#993 dam

ڈیم

#994 grocery

گروسری

#995 factory

فیکٹری

#996 supermarket

سپرمارکیٹ

#997 library

کتب خانہ

#998 shop

دکان

#999 city

شہر

#1000 lab

لیب

Made in United States
Orlando, FL
10 October 2024

52540250R00043